WILLIAM AND KATE

Prince William is one of the world's most famous young men. He comes from a very old and important family. His mother was the beautiful Princess Diana and his father is Prince Charles – the next king of England.

William is going to be king one day, too, and when you are the future king, the eyes of the world are always on you. People are interested in every part of your life – your friends, your school, your university, and of course your girlfriend.

'Who is Prince William's girlfriend?' the newspapers asked, again and again. 'What's her name?' they said. 'Is she from a royal family in a different country?'

In the end, they found the answer. And on 29 April 2011, the world smiled on the now married Duke and Duchess of Cambridge – William and Kate.

OXFORD BOOKWORMS LIBRARY
Factfiles

William and Kate

Stage 1 (400 headwords)

Factfiles Series Editor: Christine Lindop

CHRISTINE LINDOP

William and Kate

OXFORD UNIVERSITY PRESS

OXFORD
UNIVERSITY PRESS

Great Clarendon Street, Oxford, OX2 6DP, United Kingdom

Oxford University Press is a department of the University of Oxford.
It furthers the University's objective of excellence in research, scholarship,
and education by publishing worldwide. Oxford is a registered trade
mark of Oxford University Press in the UK and in certain other countries

© Oxford University Press 2013

The moral rights of the author have been asserted

First published 2013

10 9 8 7 6 5 4

ISBN: 978 0 19 423668 3

A complete recording of *William and Kate* is available on CD. Pack ISBN: 978 0 19 423660 7

Printed in China

Word count (main text): 5,132

For more information on the Oxford Bookworms Library,
visit www.oup.com/elt/gradedreaders

ACKNOWLEDGEMENTS

Cover image: Duke and Duchess of Cambridge journey by carriage/Peter Macdiarmid.
The publishers would like to thank the following for their permission to reproduce photographs: Camera
Press p.11 (Kate at school/Mark Stewart/Pool); Corbis pp.8 (Prince William during his gap year/
Reuters), 17 (Prince William with RAF mountain rescue/Ian Hodgson/Reuters), 21 (Concert for
Diana 2007/Stephen Hird/Reuters), 21 (Concert for Diana 2007/Hubert Boesl/dpa), 22 (Prince
William as co-pilot/MOD Crown Copy 2011/dpa), 23 (Zebra at waterhole, Kenya/Tui De Roy/
Minden Pictures), 26 (Royal wedding invitation/John Stillwell/epa), 36 (The Seychelles/Frank
Lukasseck), 37 (William and Kate on official visit to Canada/Splash News), 38 (Duke and
Duchess of Cambridge at charity gala/Facundo Arrizabalaga/epa), 44 (Married couple/Erica
Shires), 44 (Bridesmaid/Jim Craigmyle/First Light), 44 (Bride/Corry/ClassicStock), 44 (Queen
Elizabeth II/Pool Photograph); Getty Images pp.0 (Spectators near Westminster Abbey/Sean
Gallup), 1 (William and Harry arriving for wedding/Dan Kitwood), 2 (The Royal Family 1972/
Lichfield), 4 (The Middleton family/Ian Gavan/GP), 6 (Prince William's first day at Eton/Tim
Graham), 12 (Students at St Andrew's University/Jeff J Mitchell), 13 (Kate in Fashion show/M
Neilson), 15 (Kate skiing/Tim Graham), 15 (Prince Charles and family in Klosters/Pascal Le
Segretain), 16 (Prince William's graduation/Tim Graham), 16 (New graduate Kate Middleton/
Tim Graham), 22 (Prince William with search and rescue crew/WPA Pool), 29 (Catherine
Middleton in wedding dress/Pascal Le Segretain), 30 (Wedding ceremony/Andrew Milligan/
AFP), 33 (Kate and William official wedding photo/2011 St James's Palace, by photographer
Hugo Burnand), 34 (McVities chocolate cake), 44 (Prince Harry greets crowds/James Devaney/
FilmMagic); Oxford University Press 44 (Teen couple/Westend61); Press Association Images
p.27 (Camilla, Duchess of Cornwall, greets public/AP Photo/Joel Ryan); Rex Features
pp.3 (Diana and Charles with sons/Nick Skinner), 5 (Princess Diana and Prince Charles with
Prince William, 1983/News Ltd/Newspix), 5 (Kensington Palace/Anders Good/IBL), 9 (Kate
Middleton and family/© The Middleton Family, 2011), 10 (Kate Middleton, aged 3/© The
Middleton Family, 2011), 10 (A young Kate/© The Middleton Family, 2011), 18 (The Queen
and Prince William at The Parade of Sandhurst/Jeremy Selwyn/Evening Standard), 19 (Kate in
early 2007/Tony Kyriacou), 20 (Pippa and Kate Middleton), 23 (Kate Middleton's engagement
ring/Tim Rooke), 24 (Prince William's Engagement To Kate Middleton/David Crump/Daily
Mail), 25 (Westminster Abbey/Monkey Business), 26 (Preparations for the Royal Wedding/
Paul Grover), 28 (Wedding guests David and Victoria Beckham/Willi Schneider), 31 (Duke
and Duchess of Cambridge in horse-drawn carriage/Jane Mingay), 32 (William and Kate
balcony kiss/Paul Grover), 34 (The Duke and Duchess of Cambridge's royal wedding cake),
39 (Centrepoint's 40th Anniversary reception); TRH The Duke and Duchess of Cambridge
2013, p.40

CONTENTS

1   The big day begins

The sun is coming up over London, and the city is coming alive. There are always lots of visitors in London, but today something is different. On the Mall, some of the visitors are sleeping in chairs near the road, and others are standing and talking. More and more people are walking, driving, and taking trains into the city. They come from towns and cities all over the UK, and from other countries too.

Later in the morning, in the Goring Hotel in Belgravia, a young woman is getting ready for a very special day. Her parents, her sister, and her brother are there in the hotel with her. She must do her hair and face, and then put on a very special dress. Everyone wants to know about her dress – but they must wait.

At the same time, not far away, a young man is getting ready too. He and his brother put on their uniforms – red for him, black for his brother. They laugh and talk together.

The young woman is Kate Middleton, and the young man is Prince William – one day the king of the United Kingdom. Today is their wedding day. And on this day, two very different families come together – the royal family, and the Middleton family.

Prince William and Prince Harry in uniform

2   Two families

William comes from a very important family, and his grandmother is one of the richest and most famous women in the world. She is Queen Elizabeth the Second, Queen of the United Kingdom of Great Britain and Northern Ireland, and of fifteen other countries. She is married to Prince Philip, and they have four children: three sons and a daughter.

From left to right: Princess Anne, Prince Charles, Prince Edward, Prince Andrew, Queen Elizabeth, and Prince Philip in 1972

Prince Charles and Princess Diana with William and Harry in 1987

The Queen's oldest son, Prince Charles, is William's father. His mother was a very famous woman too. She was Princess Diana. William was born in 1982. He was Charles and Diana's first child. They had a second son, Prince Harry, in 1984.

Because he is part of the royal family, William is always in the public eye. Photographers, newspaper reporters, and TV cameras are part of his everyday life. When he was a child, his home was a big palace with many rooms, and beautiful gardens. And he lives in a palace now for some of the time too.

Kate comes from a very different family. Her parents are Michael and Carole Middleton. They met when they worked for British Airways. Kate is their oldest child, and she has a sister, Pippa, and a brother, James. When Kate was six years old, Carole Middleton began a business called Party Pieces, and later Michael Middleton worked in the business with her. It made a lot of money for the family – but they do not live in a palace!

Two young people – one is from a royal family, and the other is not. Many years ago, a marriage like this could not happen. But more royal weddings in countries around the world are like this now. For example, in 2005, Prince Felipe of Spain married Letizia Ortiz Rocasolano.

Before she married him, she was a TV reporter. And in the same year Princess Sayako of Japan left the Japanese royal family when she married Yoshiki Kuroda. Today's princes and princesses do not always marry people from royal families.

Carole, James, Michael, and Pippa Middleton

3   A young prince

William Arthur Philip Louis was born in London on 21 June 1982. He lived at Kensington Palace with his parents, Prince Charles and Princess Diana. When he was only nine months old, his parents made an official visit to Australia and New Zealand. His mother did not want to be away from William for six weeks, so the little prince went with his parents. Before he could walk or talk, William began to go around the world.

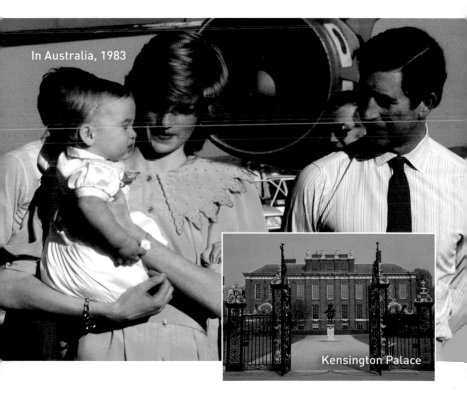

In Australia, 1983

Kensington Palace

William in his
school uniform at
Eton College in 1995

William's brother Harry was born two years later, in 1984. The two little boys enjoyed playing together at the palace. Young children in the royal family usually had lessons at home, but Princess Diana changed things. When William was three years old, he began to go to school in London with other young children.

When he was eight, he went to Ludgrove School, about 60 kilometres away from London. He lived at the school, and only went home once a month. At first he was unhappy, but he soon began to enjoy football and other sports. Later, his brother Harry came to the school too.

But things were not good at home, and in December 1992 there was bad news. Princess Diana came to see William at his school. She and Prince Charles were not a couple any more. William was very unhappy about this.

In 1995, William went to the famous Eton College. It is near Windsor Castle, so William could go there and see his grandmother, the Queen, from time to time. William worked well at school, and was good at football and other sports.

Then on 31 August 1997, there was terrible news for William. His mother, the beautiful Princess Diana, was dead after a very bad car accident in Paris. On 6 September, William walked behind his mother's body through the streets of London to Westminster Abbey. Prince Harry, Prince Charles, Prince Philip, and Diana's brother Earl Spencer walked with him. Everyone felt sorry for the two young princes. It was a terrible day for the British royal family.

William left Eton in the summer of 2000, but he did not go to university at once. He had a gap year – a year between school and university. He did a lot of different things in his gap year, and some of them were not very usual for a prince. He went to Chile for ten weeks and worked as a teacher. After work every day, he cleaned the rooms and cooked with the other teachers. He also helped to make new buildings. Later, he also worked in England on a farm with animals; he got up very early in the morning, and he did not get very much money for his work.

At the end of summer 2001, William was ready to go to university. He wanted to learn about art history. On a sunny September day in 2001, Prince Charles drove his son not to Oxford or Cambridge, but north to Scotland. Thousands of people waited in a little Scottish town to see the young prince when he arrived. He was now a student at the University of St Andrews.

William working in Chile

4   Kate's early years

Catherine Elizabeth Middleton (very often called Kate) was born on 9 January 1982 in Reading in the south of England – so she is five months older than William. Her sister Pippa was born the next year. In 1984, her father's work took him to Amman in Jordan, so Michael and Carole Middleton went to live there for two years with their two young daughters.

Kate, her sister, and her father in Jordan in 1985

In 1986, they came back to England to their home in Berkshire in the village of Bradfield Southend. Kate began school here and enjoyed playing with her sister and children in the village. Her brother James, the last of the Middletons' three children, was born in April 1987.

Kate did well at her school work, but she also enjoyed doing sport. She was good at tennis and hockey and she liked running too. In 1995, her family moved to a new home near Bucklebury, but Kate was not there for very long. She went away from home to Marlborough College in Wiltshire. At first she wanted to be at home with her family, but then she began to make friends. She played in hockey and tennis teams for the school, and she did very well in her lessons too. Now she was a beautiful young woman, and she enjoyed her last months at Marlborough. She left in July 2000.

Like William, she did not go to university that year. She had a gap year too. First she went to Florence, in Italy, for three months. Florence is famous for its art, and Kate went to see a lot of pictures in the city. She also learned Italian, went out with friends, and enjoyed taking photographs.

Kate at five years old

Kate at three

Kate at school in 1990

After Christmas at home with her family, Kate went to Chile – just like William. His visit was from October to December 2000, and she went there in January 2001 – so they did not meet. She helped to make a new building and she also worked as a teacher for a time. And then, back in England, Kate got ready to go to St Andrews as a student of art history.

No photographers waited at her Berkshire home when she left there in September 2001. No television cameras photographed her when she arrived at the University of St Andrews. But it was the beginning of a very different life for Kate.

5   St Andrews

The little town of St Andrews is next to the sea in the east of Scotland. It is very famous for golf. People began to play golf there in the 1500s, or perhaps earlier. Now golfers come from all over the world to play there.

The University of St Andrews is very old. It first opened in 1413, and it is the oldest university in Scotland, and the third oldest in the UK after Oxford and Cambridge. It has more than 8,000 students.

The beginning of the university year was very different for Kate and William. Kate was soon busy with student life, and she enjoyed Raisin Weekend. This is a special weekend at the university. On these two days in November, a new student meets their student 'mother' and 'father'. These older students help them in their first year.

Raisin Weekend at St Andrews University

Kate in a coloured jumper at the fashion show

Everybody enjoys these two noisy days. But William's first weeks at the university were very quiet.

William and Kate lived in the same building, were students of art history, and had some of the same friends. In March 2002, Kate was in a fashion show at the university, and William and some friends went to watch. Girls in wonderful dresses walked up and down. Kate came out in a beautiful coloured jumper at first, but then she walked out in a very exciting black dress, and she looked wonderful! (In 2011, the designer got £78,000 for the dress!) Soon, William and Kate were friends. Later, William said, 'We were friends for over a year first.'

In their second year, many students do not live at the university. They find a flat or house in the town and live there together. William and some friends did this in 2002. The four friends cleaned the flat and did some of the cooking. Sometimes William began to cook dinner for Kate there – but often things went wrong, and then Kate finished cooking for them.

In the summer of 2003, Kate was twenty-one, and William went to a party at her parents' house in Berkshire. Other friends from St Andrews were there too. Later, Prince Charles had an 'African' party for William's twenty-first birthday at Windsor Castle. It was not an official party, with suits and speeches. The guests wore African clothes, and African musicians played for them. Kate was one of the guests at the party.

In September 2003, they began their third year at university. Now, William moved to a house in the country called Balgove House. It was not far from the town and the university, but it was a quiet place, away from photographers and reporters.

Then in March 2004, William and Kate were in the news – together. They went to Klosters in Switzerland on a skiing holiday with some friends, and William's father Prince Charles. Soon, newspapers all over the world had a photo of William with Kate. Now everybody wanted to know 'Who is Kate Middleton?' The newspapers started to write about 'Will and Kate' as a couple.

September 2004 was the beginning of their last year at St Andrews. There were often photos of William at weddings and parties without Kate. She was not part of

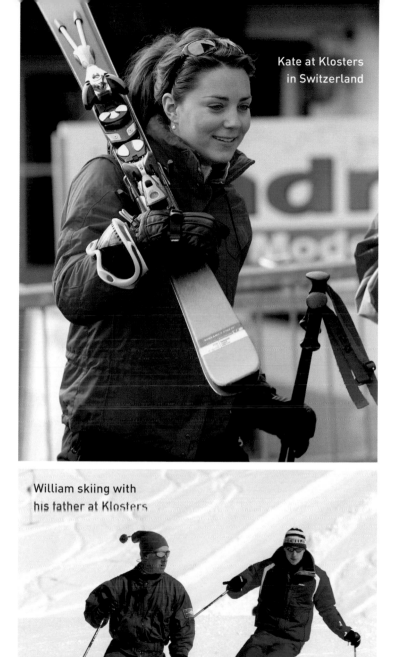

Kate at Klosters
in Switzerland

William skiing with
his father at Klosters

the royal family, so she could not always go with him. But they were boyfriend and girlfriend.

Then in June 2005, they graduated from St Andrews. The Queen, Prince Philip, and Prince Charles all came up to Scotland for the special ceremony. Kate's mother and father were there too, but the two families did not meet.

It was the end of William and Kate's happy university life. But what was next for these two young people?

Graduation day
at St Andrews

6 Together – and after

Now a new life began for William and Kate – a more public life. Soon after graduation, William went to New Zealand for the second time. It was his first official visit to a country, and he stayed there for eleven days.

Then it was time for a holiday. William went to Lewa Downs in Kenya and stayed there for a month. Later, Kate and some of their friends went there for a holiday with him. But the holiday in this quiet beautiful place was soon over.

William began to have a very busy time. He worked in the City of London and learned about banks. He also worked at the Football Association and at Chatsworth House, a big country house in Derbyshire in the north of England. In December, he spent two weeks with a mountain rescue team. After a skiing holiday at Klosters in January 2006, Kate and William said goodbye. William went to Sandhurst to learn to be an army officer, and stayed there for forty-four weeks. Like all the other officers, William needed to do a lot of work, and he did not see Kate very often.

Things were not easy for Kate. She needed to find work – but she was the girlfriend of a prince. Photographers

William with the mountain rescue team

William at his Sandhurst graduation
with his grandmother Queen Elizabeth

ran after her in the street and waited near her house. For a
lot of the time she worked in her parents' business; there
she could get away from the newspapers. In November
2006, she began work with a women's clothes business
called Jigsaw – it has shops in many bigger towns in
the UK.

The next month, William graduated from Sandhurst,
and Kate and her parents were at the ceremony. But in
2007, things did not get better.

Life is not easy when you are the wife, husband,
girlfriend, or boyfriend of someone in the royal family.
Reporters and photographers from the newspapers and
the TV watch you all the time. You cannot go out of the
house in old clothes – you must always look your best.

Every walk in the street and every visit to the shops can be in the newspapers. Not everyone can live like this, and couples in the public eye often stop being together. Of the Queen's four children, only the youngest, Prince Edward, is in his first marriage.

At twenty-four, William was not ready to get married. He was very busy in the army in Dorset, and Kate worked a hundred miles away in London. Sometimes there were pictures in the newspapers of William with other girls too. In April 2007, the news came at last. William and Kate were not boyfriend and girlfriend any more. Kate went back to live at her parents' house, away from London and the cameras.

Kate in early 2007

7 Together again

But Kate did not stay at home for long. Soon she was back in London, and she often went out with her sister Pippa.

William was busy too. His mother, Princess Diana, was born on 1 July 1961, and he and his brother Harry wanted to have a concert for her on 1 July. On that day, 63,000 people came to the concert, with singers like Elton John, Rod Stewart, and P. Diddy, and millions watched it on TV around the world. And there was an important guest at the concert too – Kate Middleton. She did not sit

Kate goes shopping with Pippa

At the concert – William and Harry ...

... and Kate and her brother

next to William, but she was not far away. And she had a happy smile on her face. After two months, they were back together again.

Next month, Kate and William flew to the beautiful islands of the Seychelles for a week. This time, no friends came with them on their holiday. But their visit was over quickly, and they were soon back to the busy world of work.

William spent twelve weeks with the Royal Air Force (RAF) and learned to fly. Kate was at the ceremony when he graduated. Then he had two months with the Royal Navy. In autumn 2008, he went to the RAF again, and this time he learned to fly a helicopter. His father Prince Charles, his brother Prince Harry, and his father's brother Prince Andrew can all fly helicopters, and William wanted very much to do so too.

William with
his search and
rescue team

Kate worked for her parents' business and sometimes took photographs for them. The newspapers watched and waited. There were many photos of Kate, and lots of people were interested in her clothes. 'Beautiful!' said some, but 'Not very exciting!' said others.

In January 2010, William finished his helicopter training. He then went to the beautiful island of Anglesey in North Wales to train with the RAF in search and rescue work. He lived in a little house on a farm, and Kate often visited him.

William's training in search and rescue ended in September 2010, and soon after that he and Kate went to Kenya for a three-week holiday. It was the end of William's training – and the beginning of a new life for the two of them.

8   The engagement

For some of the time in Kenya, William and Kate were with friends. But near the end of the holiday they had some time together. Kate did not know it, but in his bag William had a very special ring. It was his mother's engagement ring   a beautiful gold ring with a big blue sapphire and little diamonds. William carried it carefully in his bag all through the holiday. Then, on 19 October 2010, he asked Kate to marry him, and he gave her the ring. Kate, of course, said yes.

The ring

The young couple came back to the UK, but they could not tell the exciting news to their friends, and Kate could not wear the ring. In public, they lived their usual lives and did not talk about their engagement.

Kenya

16 November 2010

At last, on 16 November, the couple came on TV at St James's Palace in London, and the news was out. They were engaged. Kate wore a beautiful blue dress, the same colour as the sapphire in her ring. The two young people looked very happy.

William talked about his mother's ring. Of course, his mother Princess Diana died in 1997. But for him, his mother was 'there' at the engagement because of the ring.

William asked Kate to marry him – but he asked two other people about the wedding. He asked Kate's father Michael Middleton, soon after he asked Kate. And he asked the Queen. A royal prince or princess must ask the Queen before they can marry. Happily, Michael Middleton said yes, and the Queen did too.

And of course there were lots of questions. Where is the wedding going to be? Who is coming? And for a lot of people the most important question: what is the bride going to wear?

9 Getting ready

Now the question was not 'Are they going to get married?' but 'When are they going to get married?'

The answer came a week later. The wedding day was Friday 29 April 2011 in Westminster Abbey.

Of course, there was now a lot to do. Firstly, there was the question of the guests. The most important person in the royal family – the Queen – asked about 1,900 people to the wedding. Many of these were family and friends, but she also asked other kings and queens from countries around the world.

Westminster Abbey

A wedding ring was made for Kate from Welsh gold. William's mother Diana had a wedding ring of Welsh gold – and his grandmother Queen Elizabeth and her mother did too.

A bride needs bridesmaids. These young women help her with her dress and flowers. And a groom needs a special helper too – he is called a best man. William's brother Harry was his best man, and Kate's sister Pippa

Workers bring trees into the abbey before the wedding

EⅡR

The Lord Chamberlain is commanded by
The Queen to invite

_____

_____

to the Marriage of
His Royal Highness Prince William of Wales, K.G.
with
Miss Catherine Middleton
at Westminster Abbey
on Friday, 29th April, 2011 at 11.00 a.m.

Dress: Uniform, Morning Coat
or Lounge Suit

ply is requested to:
tate Invitations Secretary, Lord Chamberlain's Office,
Buckingham Palace, London SW1A 1AA

was her most important bridesmaid. Then there were four other little girls and two little boys. The children were from the royal family or from the families of William's friends.

Then there was the cake and the flowers (William and Kate had eight trees in the abbey too!) but of course everybody wanted to know about the bride's dress. 'Who is going to make it?' they asked.

The months went quickly by, and soon it was April. On Thursday 28 April, thousands of people began to arrive in London. They waited near Westminster Abbey and on the Mall, because they wanted to see everything on Friday morning. But there were some famous visitors to the Mall that night.

First, Prince Charles's second wife, the Duchess of Cornwall, came and talked to people. 'We're all ready for tomorrow – it's wonderful and we're all very excited!' she said. And later, Prince William came out and talked to people too. He looked happy, and said 'Hello' and 'Thank you' to the visitors. Lots of people took photos. Now there was just one night before the wedding.

The Duchess of Cornwall with visitors in the Mall

10 The wedding

And so the day of the royal wedding began. It was a warm day, with no rain. Hundreds of thousands of people waited on the streets, and 5,000 police officers were at work. In different parts of London, there were more than 8,000 radio and TV reporters from different countries, ready to tell people around the world about the wedding.

At 8 a.m., there was news from Buckingham Palace. William and Kate had new titles – the Duke and Duchess of Cambridge. So Kate was now a duchess – but not a princess.

Then guests began to arrive at Westminster Abbey. People on the street looked for famous guests. 'Look, there's David and Victoria Beckham.' 'Isn't that Elton John?' 'Look at Princess Beatrice's hat!' There were famous people, beautiful clothes – and lots of interesting hats.

Guests David and Victoria Beckham

Near to 10.30, William and Harry came into the abbey. Soon after that, Kate's mother arrived, and then the Queen and Prince Philip. Then, at 10.51, people saw Kate for the first time when she left the hotel and got into a Rolls-Royce car with her father. And ten minutes later, she arrived at the famous abbey, and everyone could see her clothes for the first time. 'What a beautiful dress!' the TV reporters said excitedly. 'And it's by a British designer called Sarah Burton.'

In Westminster Abbey,
after the ceremony

The dress was white, with a big skirt and long lace sleeves. Kate wore a white veil over her face and a diamond tiara on her head. In her hands she carried small white flowers and on her feet she had beautiful wedding shoes.

Kate walked slowly into the abbey with her father. Her sister Pippa walked behind, and she carefully carried the train – the long part at the back of the dress. Pippa wore a special white dress too.

There were hundreds of white and green flowers in the Abbey, and there were eight tall trees. Kate and her father walked past all the guests and then Kate stood next to William. 'You look beautiful,' he said to his bride.

The ceremony took a little more than an hour. Then the new Duke and Duchess of Cambridge walked out of the abbey with Prince Harry, Pippa, the six children, Kate's parents, Prince Charles, and the Duchess of Cornwall.

The bride and groom got into an open gold and black carriage to go back to Buckingham Palace. Everybody could see Kate's beautiful dress and the couple's happy smiles. The other important guests from the royal

Driving to Buckingham Palace

family, and Carole and Michael Middleton, drove behind in different carriages.

After the carriages arrived at the palace, thousands of people began to walk along the Mall to the palace. Police officers walked slowly in front of them. Then everyone watched the balcony and waited for the royal couple.

A royal bride and groom first came onto the balcony at Buckingham Palace in 1858. William's parents, Prince Charles and Princess Diana, famously kissed on the balcony in 1981. So when Kate and William came onto the balcony, everyone called, 'Kiss, kiss, kiss!' They smiled and kissed – and later they kissed again. There was a lot of noise. One little bridesmaid, three years old, put her hands over her ears!

Then there were photographs – of the bride and groom together, and with their families. And after that, a party

William and Kate
kiss on the balcony

The couple with their bridesmaids and other helpers

– for 650 people! The guests were in nineteen rooms at the palace. The royal couple met a lot of the guests, and Prince Charles made a speech.

And there were two wedding cakes. One was a big white cake. It was made from seventeen different cakes, and it had hundreds of flowers on it. And Prince William asked for a second cake – a chocolate cake. When William was a boy, his grandmother gave him this cake at Windsor Castle on his visits from Eton.

That evening, there was a dinner for 300 guests at Buckingham Palace. The guests sat at tables with the

The special chocolate cake

The big wedding cake

names of Kate and William's special places, like Lewa in Kenya and St Andrews. There were speeches from Prince Harry, Michael Middleton, and Prince William, and from two of William's friends. And then the party began. In one of the biggest rooms in the palace, guests talked and danced into the morning. At 3 a.m. the bride and groom left, and the party ended.

Of course, the party at the palace was not the only party in the UK. The day of the wedding was a holiday, and there were more than 5,000 street parties. In St Andrews, more than 2,000 people came together to have a party and to watch the wedding on a big TV. David Cameron, the British Prime Minister, had a party near his house in Downing Street for older people and schoolchildren, and his wife made cakes for the party. In cities and towns across the UK, people closed their streets and came together for the day. They ate, drank, talked, and watched the wedding together.

And there were parties in other places too. In 180 countries, many millions of people watched the pictures from London. From Afghanistan to China, and from India to Canada, many people watched the wedding with their friends or families. In Times Square in New York City, three couples got married just after William and Kate. But in New York City, of course, it was 6 a.m. when the royal wedding began, so the weddings in Times Square were very early in the morning!

It was a wonderful day for William and Kate – and around the world, millions of people enjoyed it with them.

11 And after

Many couples have a honeymoon – a holiday together after their wedding. 'Where are William and Kate going to go on honeymoon?' people asked. But there was no news from Buckingham Palace.

On Saturday 30 April, the day after the wedding, William and Kate left Buckingham Palace in a helicopter. But after three days away, they went back to Anglesey. On Tuesday, William was back at work with the search and rescue team.

Ten days after the wedding, William and Kate flew to the Seychelles for ten days. On the quiet islands they could have more time together and enjoy the sun, away from reporters and photographers.

The Seychelles

Then it was back to Anglesey – and a new life for Kate in the royal family. And before long they had their first visit as a royal couple – to Canada, from 30 June to 8 July. Thousands of people came to see the young couple. William and Kate went to official ceremonies, but they also talked to a lot of people, young and old. And William gave speeches in English and French.

Talking to children in Canada

When they left Canada, they went to California for three days. At a big dinner in Los Angeles, they met Jennifer Lopez, Nicole Kidman, and other people from the cinema. But they also spent time at Inner-City Arts. Children from families with little money go there to have lessons in dance and art. The Duke and Duchess watched the dances and made pictures with the children.

On these visits, reporters are often very interested in Kate – her hair, her shoes, and her dresses. Sometimes, she wears clothes from special designers, but she often wears things from British shops. Of course, when some young women see Kate in a beautiful new dress, they go to the nearest big city and get the same dress. Often these 'Kate' dresses all go from the shops in two or three hours! So Kate is very good news for some British clothes businesses.

What next for the young couple? William has his work with the search and rescue team. And William and Kate must also make visits and go to ceremonies, because they are part of the royal family. These official visits are often to places far from Britain – like Malaysia, Singapore, or the Solomon Islands. Here the couple can learn about the lives of different people – an important thing for a future king and queen.

Of course, many organizations ask for help from people in the royal family. Prince William helps a mountain rescue organization, and he often does work for the Football Association too. When William was a child, he sometimes visited special places for people without homes in London – these were part of the Centrepoint organization. Centrepoint was always very important to his

William with young
people at Centrepoint

mother Diana, and William gives some of his time to
it too. William wanted to learn about the very different
world of people without homes, so in December 2009, he
slept on the cold streets of London for one night.

The Duchess now helps four organizations too. One
of the organizations is called East Anglia Children's
Hospice; it helps very ill children and their families.
One of the other organizations is the National Portrait
Gallery. This is in a big building in London and it has
thousands of pictures of people. Of course, Kate knows
a lot about art history and she enjoys working with this
organization.

The Duke and Duchess of Cambridge also helped
the people in the British Olympic Games team in the
summer of 2012. It was a very busy time for the British
royal family – they went to the big Olympic ceremonies

in London and they talked to many famous visitors from countries around the world.

When they got engaged, Kate said, 'Family is very important to me.' On 22 July 2013, their son George was born, and on 2 May 2015, their daughter Charlotte was born. It is not an easy life in the royal family, but perhaps Kate, William, George, and Charlotte can have a happy future – everybody hopes so. And of course, they are going to be in the news for many years to come.

GLOSSARY

also   too; as well

army   a group of people who fight for their country

around   in different places; all the way round

art history   the study of pictures and artists from the past

beginning   when something begins

business   buying and selling things; a place where people
      sell things

busy   with a lot of things to do

ceremony   an important time when people come to a special
      place or building to do traditional things

city   a big and important town

clean   to stop something being dirty

clothes   things you wear, e.g. shirts, trousers, dresses

concert   music played for a lot of people

cook   to make things for people to eat

couple   two people who are married or going to get married

dance   to move your body to music

designer   a person who draws clothes and shows how they can
      be made

end   (*n & v*) to stop, to finish something

get engaged   to agree to get married; (*n*) engagement

enjoy   to like something very much

farm   a place where people keep animals and grow food

flat   a number of rooms in a building where people live

fly   (past **flew**) to go to a different place in an aeroplane

future   what is going to happen

graduate   to finish your studies at university; (*n*) **graduation**

guest   a person that you invite to a party or wedding etc.

holiday   a time when you travel to another place for pleasure

island   a piece of land with water around it

life   the time that you are alive; the way that you live

marriage   the time when two people are together as husband
      and wife

marry / (get) married   to take somebody as your husband
   or wife
mountain rescue   a team of people who help walkers when they
   are hurt or lost in the mountains
news   stories about things that are happening now
newspaper   people read about things that happen every day
   in this
officer   a person in the army who is in charge of other people
official   when something is of the government and very
   important
organization   a group of people all working for something
other   different
over   finished
parent   a mother or father
part   one of the pieces of something
party   a meeting of friends, to eat, drink and dance
place   where something or somebody is
police officer   a man or woman who stops people doing
   bad things
public   open to everyone
reporter   a person who writes for a newspaper or speaks on
   the TV
royal   of or about a king or queen
same   not different
search and rescue   a team of people who help others when they
   are hurt or lost in a dangerous place like the sea
special   not usual or ordinary
speech   a talk that you give to a lot of people
team   a group of people who play a sport against another group
terrible   very bad
together   with another person
train   to learn how to do a new job; *(n)* **training**
unhappy   not happy
university   a place where people study after leaving school
wedding   the time when two people marry
world   the earth with all its countries and people

William and Kate

ACTIVITIES

ACTIVITIES

Before Reading

1 **Complete the table with the words.**

best man, boyfriend, bride, bridesmaid, girlfriend, groom, ~~king~~, queen, prince, princess

	Male	Female
The most important person in a country	king	
The son or daughter of a king		
A person on their wedding day		
An important helper at a wedding		
A person who is a special friend		

2 **Now match six of the words from exercise 1 to the pictures.**

1 _____   2 _____   3 _____

4 _____   5 _____   6 _____

ACTIVITIES

While Reading

Read Chapters 1 and 2, then fill in the gaps.

1 On the day of the wedding, _____ slept on the Mall.

2 _____ got ready for the wedding in the Goring Hotel.

3 _____ wore a black uniform to the wedding.

4 Prince William is the grandson of _____.

5 Prince William's parents were _____ and Prince Charles.

6 In 1984, _____'s younger brother was born.

7 _____ first met his wife at work.

8 _____ opened the Party Pieces business.

9 _____'s wife was once a reporter on television.

10 When _____ got married, she left the royal family.

Read Chapter 3, then put these sentences in the right order.

1 Prince William went to Australia with his parents.

2 Prince William went to Ludgrove School.

3 Princess Diana died suddenly in France.

4 Prince William was born in London.

5 Charles and Diana stopped being a couple.

6 William left school and took a gap year.

7 Prince Charles took William to St Andrews University.

8 William began to study at Eton College.

9 Princess Diana sent William to a school for little children in London.

Read Chapters 4, then circle *a*, *b*, or *c*.

1 Kate Middleton was born in _____.
  a) Amman   b) Bucklebury   c) Reading

2 Prince William is _____ than Kate.
  a) younger   b) older   c) smaller

3 When Kate was young she could ____ well.
  a) sing   b) play tennis   c) cook

4 Kate didn't feel _____ when she started at Marlborough.
  a) well   b) happy   c) interested

5 Kate visited ____ first on her gap year.
  a) Chile   b) Jordan   c) Italy

6 At St Andrews University Kate studied ____.
  a) art history   b) Italian   c) teaching

Read Chapter 5. Then match these halves of sentences.

1 People first played golf in St Andrews . . .

2 St Andrews University began . . .

3 'Raisin Weekend' happens every year . . .

4 Kate wore a black dress . . .

5 William went to a special party . . .

6 Photographers took a picture of William with Kate . . .

7 The Queen came to St Andrews . . .

a in the month of November.

b when William graduated.

c at Kate's parents' house.

d in the 1500s.

e at a university fashion show.

f in 1413.

g in Switzerland.

Read Chapter 6. Choose the best question-word for these questions, and then answer them.
How many / What / Who / Where / Why

1 . . . did William go to on his first official visit?
2 . . . did William do after his visit to Kenya?
3 . . . did William train to be at Sandhurst?
4 . . . weeks did William spend at Sandhurst?
5 . . . did Kate work for at first?
6 . . . could William and Kate not meet very often in 2007?'
7 . . . happened in April 2007?

Read Chapters 7 and 8, then rewrite these untrue sentences with the correct information.

1 At the Princess Diana concert, Kate sat next to William.
2 William learned to drive a car in autumn 2008.
3 William trained with the RAF on an island in Scotland.
4 Kate and William went to Kenya on an official visit.
5 William gave Kate a special letter in Kenya.
6 The couple told the good news to their friends at once.
7 On 16 November 2010, Kate put on a beautiful green dress.
8 William needed to ask Prince Charles before he could marry.

Read Chapter 9, then answer these questions.

1 When and where was the wedding?
2 How many people did the Queen ask to the wedding?
3 What was Kate's wedding ring made from?
4 Who were Kate and William's most important helpers?
5 Where did visitors to London wait before the wedding?
6 Who talked to people in the Mall before the wedding?

Read Chapter 10. Are these sentences true (T) or false (F)? Rewrite the false ones with the correct information.

1 It rained on the morning of the wedding.
2 Kate's new name was the Princess of Cambridge.
3 The footballer David Beckham came to the wedding.
4 Kate wore a beautiful white dress by a British designer.
5 The flowers in the abbey were lots of different colours.
6 William and Kate went to the palace in an open car.
7 The couple had more than one kiss on the balcony.
8 At the party, there were seventeen wedding cakes.
9 William and Kate left the party at 3 a.m.
10 In St Andrews a lot of people went to a big party.
11 Thousands of people around the world watched the
    wedding.

Read Chapter 11, then fill in the gaps with these words.

*British, California, Canada, clothes, French, homes,
London, organizations, the Olympic Games, streets, ten,
the Seychelles, Singapore, three*

For their honeymoon, the couple went to _____ for
_____ days. Next, they went on a royal visit to _____ and
William gave speeches in _____ and English. They then
visited _____ for _____ days. Sometimes they need to go
to faraway places like _____ too. On all these visits, people
are interested in Kate's _____. She buys a lot of her things
from _____ shops.

    The couple also help different _____. William works
with an organization for people without _____ in _____
and he once spent the night on the _____. They also
helped with _____ in summer 2012.

ACTIVITIES

After Reading

1 Use the clues below to complete this crossword with words from the book. Then find the hidden nine-letter word.

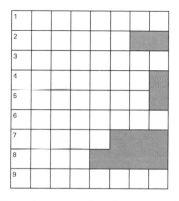

1 Kate's wedding dress was by the _____ Sarah Burton.

2 William is going to be king one day in the _____.

3 In June 2005, William's family watched him _____.

4 William and Harry had a _____ for their mother in 2007.

5 A lot of people came to London for the royal _____.

6 The _____ was in Westminster Abbey. It was an hour long.

7 William is _____ Elizabeth's grandson.

8 There was terrible _____ about Princess Diana in 1997.

9 Kate worked for her parents' party _____.

The hidden word in the crossword is _____.

What do you know about this place?

2 **Complete this postcard using the words below.**

*bride, busy, carriage, ceremony, couple, dress, enjoying,
guests, holiday, place, police officers, reporters, royal, sleeves,
together, uniforms*

LONDON   Dear Amy   Saturday 30 April BY AIR MAIL
                                                      par avion

I'm having a wonderful _____ in London and I'm really _____ my
stay here. We came on Thursday, ready for the _____ wedding
yesterday. We found a good _____ in front of Westminster Abbey so
we saw everything!
The streets of the city were very _____ – there were newspaper
and TV _____ from around the world and of course, a lot of
_____ too.
The _____ began to arrive from about 9.00. Some of them were
famous – I saw David and Victoria Beckham, and Elton John. Then at
10.30, the groom and his brother, Prince Harry, arrived _____. They
were in special _____ – William in red and Harry in black.
At about 10.50 we saw the _____ at last – she got out of
a Rolls-Royce car with her father. She was in a beautiful white
_____ with long lace _____.
The _____ finished at about 12.00 and the happy _____ drove
away in an open _____. Kate smiled at me as they went past.
I've got lots of photos and you can see them when I get back.

Love Anna x

Now imagine that you went to an important public event in
your country, for example a big concert, festival or parade.
Write a postcard to a friend about it.

3 Look back through the book again. Copy the table and make notes about William and Kate.

	William	Kate
Born – date / place		
Family – type of family, parents, brothers and sisters		
Education		
Interests		
Work		
Organizations that he or she helps		
Important days in his or her life		

Use your notes to write a short biography of William or Kate.

4 Choose a famous royal person or an important man or woman that you are interested in. Copy the grid from exercise 4 and make notes about his or her life. Then plan and give a talk about the person to your class.

ABOUT THE AUTHOR

Christine Lindop was born in New Zealand and taught English in France and Spain before settling in Great Britain. She is the Series Editor for Bookworms Factfiles, and has written or co-written more than twenty books, including several Bookworms titles – *Sally's Phone*, *Red Roses* and *The Girl with Red Hair* (Human Interest, Starter), *Ned Kelly: A True Story* (True Stories, Stage 1), and *The Bridge and other Love Stories* (Human Interest, Stage 1). For Factfiles she has written *Weddings* (Stage 1) and *Australia and New Zealand* (Stage 3). She has adapted three volumes of short stories for Bookworms World Stories: *The Long White Cloud: Stories from New Zealand* (Stage 3), *Doors to a Wider Place: Stories from Australia,* and *The Price of Peace: Stories from Africa* (Stage 4). She has also written for the Oxford Dominoes and Dolphin Readers series.

'After writing several love stories and also *Weddings*, the story of William and Kate was the perfect title for me,' she says. 'It really is the top love story of our times. What will the next chapter be? Like millions of other people, I'm looking forward to finding out.'

OXFORD BOOKWORMS LIBRARY

Classics • Crime & Mystery • Factfiles • Fantasy & Horror
Human Interest • Playscripts • Thriller & Adventure
True Stories • World Stories

The OXFORD BOOKWORMS LIBRARY provides enjoyable reading in English, with a wide range of classic and modern fiction, non-fiction, and plays. It includes original and adapted texts in seven carefully graded language stages, which take learners from beginner to advanced level. An overview is given on the next pages.

All Stage 1 titles are available as audio recordings, as well as over eighty other titles from Starter to Stage 6. All Starters and many titles at Stages 1 to 4 are specially recommended for younger learners. Every Bookworm is illustrated, and Starters and Factfiles have full-colour illustrations.

The OXFORD BOOKWORMS LIBRARY also offers extensive support. Each book contains an introduction to the story, notes about the author, a glossary, and activities. Additional resources include tests and worksheets, and answers for these and for the activities in the books. There is advice on running a class library, using audio recordings, and the many ways of using Oxford Bookworms in reading programmes. Resource materials are available on the website <www.oup.com/bookworms>.

The *Oxford Bookworms Collection* is a series for advanced learners. It consists of volumes of short stories by well-known authors, both classic and modern. Texts are not abridged or adapted in any way, but carefully selected to be accessible to the advanced student.

You can find details and a full list of titles in the *Oxford Bookworms Library Catalogue* and *Oxford English Language Teaching Catalogues*, and on the website <www.oup.com/bookworms>.

THE OXFORD BOOKWORMS LIBRARY
GRADING AND SAMPLE EXTRACTS

STARTER • 250 HEADWORDS

present simple – present continuous – imperative –
can/cannot, must – *going to* (future) – simple gerunds ...

Her phone is ringing – but where is it?

Sally gets out of bed and looks in her bag. No phone.
She looks under the bed. No phone. Then she looks behind
the door. There is her phone. Sally picks up her phone and
answers it. *Sally's Phone*

STAGE 1 • 400 HEADWORDS

... past simple – coordination with *and*, *but*, *or* –
subordination with *before*, *after*, *when*, *because*, *so* ...

I knew him in Persia. He was a famous builder and I
worked with him there. For a time I was his friend, but
not for long. When he came to Paris, I came after him –
I wanted to watch him. He was a very clever, very
dangerous man. *The Phantom of the Opera*

STAGE 2 • 700 HEADWORDS

... present perfect – *will* (future) – *(don't) have to, must not, could* –
comparison of adjectives – simple *if* clauses – past continuous –
tag questions – *ask/tell* + infinitive ...

While I was writing these words in my diary, I decided
what to do. I must try to escape. I shall try to get down the
wall outside. The window is high above the ground, but
I have to try. I shall take some of the gold with me – if I
escape, perhaps it will be helpful later. *Dracula*

STAGE 3 • 1000 HEADWORDS

... should, may – present perfect continuous – *used to* – past perfect –
causative – relative clauses – indirect statements ...

Of course, it was most important that no one should see
Colin, Mary, or Dickon entering the secret garden. So Colin
gave orders to the gardeners that they must all keep away
from that part of the garden in future. *The Secret Garden*

STAGE 4 • 1400 HEADWORDS

*... past perfect continuous – passive (simple forms) –
would* conditional clauses – indirect questions –
relatives with *where/when* – gerunds after prepositions/phrases ...

I was glad. Now Hyde could not show his face to the world
again. If he did, every honest man in London would be proud
to report him to the police. *Dr Jekyll and Mr Hyde*

STAGE 5 • 1800 HEADWORDS

*... future continuous – future perfect –
passive (modals, continuous forms) –
would have* conditional clauses – modals + perfect infinitive ...

If he had spoken Estella's name, I would have hit him. I was so
angry with him, and so depressed about my future, that I could
not eat the breakfast. Instead I went straight to the old house
Great Expectations

STAGE 6 • 2500 HEADWORDS

... passive (infinitives, gerunds) – advanced modal meanings –
clauses of concession, condition

When I stepped up to the piano, I was confident. It was as if I
knew that the prodigy side of me really did exist. And when I
started to play, I was so caught up in how lovely I looked that
I didn't worry how I would sound. *The Joy Luck Club*

BOOKWORMS · FACTFILES · STAGE 1

England

JOHN ESCOTT

Twenty-five million people come to England every year, and some never go out of London.

But England is full of interesting places to visit and things to do. There are big noisy cities with great shops and theatres, and quiet little villages. You can visit old castles and beautiful churches – or go to festivals with music twenty-four hours a day.

You can have an English afternoon tea, walk on long white beaches, watch a great game of football, or visit a country house. Yes, England has something for everybody – what has it got for you?

BOOKWORMS · FACTFILES · STAGE 1

Weddings

CHRISTINE LINDOP

'The bride wore a long white dress, with flowers in her hair. After the wedding, there was a party, and people gave presents to the bride and groom.' This wedding was nearly two thousand years ago, in Rome. Some things don't change.

But some things do. Today you can have a wedding on a mountain, or under the sea, or 'Elvis' can sing for you. And different things happen in different places. Little birds made of paper, small trees, money in the bride's shoe, and lots of noise – they are all important for weddings somewhere. Welcome to the wonderful world of weddings!